CONVERGE

Bible Studies

BEING HOLY

CONVERGE
Bible Studies

BEING HOLY

SHANE RAYNOR

Abingdon Press
Nashville

BEING HOLY
CONVERGE BIBLE STUDIES

By Shane Raynor

Copyright © 2014 by Abingdon Press

Library of Congress Cataloging-in-Publication Data has been requested.

ISBN: 978-1-4267-9552-7

Series Editor: Shane Raynor

14 15 16 17 18 19 20 21 22 23—10 9 8 7 6 5 4 3 2 1

Manufactured in the United States of America

CONTENTS

ABOUT THE SERIES

Converge is a series of topical Bible studies based on the Common English Bible translation. Each title in the *Converge* series consists of four studies based around a common topic or theme. *Converge* brings together a unique group of writers from different backgrounds, traditions, and age groups.

HOW TO USE THESE STUDIES

Converge Bible studies can be used by small groups, classes, or individuals. Each study uses a simple format. For the convenience of the reader, the primary Scripture passages are included. In Insight and Ideas, the author of the study explores each Scripture passage, going deeper into the text and helping readers understand how the Scripture connects with the theme of the study. Questions are designed to encourage both personal reflection and group conversation. Some questions may not have simple answers. That's part of what makes studying the Bible so exciting.

Although Bible passages are included with each session, study participants may find it useful to have personal Bibles on hand for referencing other Scriptures. *Converge* studies are designed for use with the Common English Bible; but they work well with any modern, reliable translation.

ONLINE EXTRAS

Converge studies are available in both print and digital formats. Each title in the series has additional components that are available online, including related blog posts and podcasts.

To access the companion materials, visit

http://www.MinistryMatters.com/Converge

Thanks for using *Converge*!

INTRODUCTION

What do you picture when you hear the word *holiness*? Some Christians think of behavior-based religion. *How is a Christian supposed to act? What would Jesus do? What are the dos and don'ts of the Christian faith? Where are the boundaries?*

The big problem, however, with focusing on behavior is that it misses the point of living faith. In Western culture, where we're heavily influenced by the business world, we tend to focus on performance; and performance has to *measurable*. A strangely warmed heart isn't measurable—neither is the infilling of the Holy Spirit—but the number of sins we commit and the amount of time we spend in prayer and Bible study are.

So we gravitate toward focusing on the things we can mentally track on our spiritual scorecards. Unfortunately, we can do everything right (although odds are we won't) and not make an ounce of progress in our walk with Christ.

When I was a church youth worker, I struggled to find that magical middle ground between cheap grace and legalism. And I discovered that if I focused too much on behavior and not enough on Jesus, students would follow my lead and do the same. Unfortunately, rather than making disciples who had freedom in Christ and lived to please God, I sometimes felt like I was giving them rules for not disappointing *me* and for fitting into the *Christian* world better.

If a desire for holiness starts with performance and behavior and doesn't come from a place of grace and relationship, then living a holy life isn't about becoming more like Christ; it's an existence that lives at the extremes of never being good enough or looking for loopholes in the Law. Our behavior has then become the *basis* for our faith (or lack of it) rather than the *fruit* of it. That's a depressing (and theologically dangerous) place to be.

Jesus had some strong words to those who focused on the external first instead of the internal:

> "How terrible it will be for you legal experts and Pharisees! Hypocrites! You clean the outside of the cup and plate, but inside they are full of violence and pleasure seeking. Blind Pharisee! First clean the inside of the cup so that the outside of the cup will be clean too.
>
> "How terrible it will be for you legal experts and Pharisees! Hypocrites! You are like whitewashed tombs. They look beautiful on the outside. But inside they are full of dead bones and all kinds of filth. In the same way you look righteous

to people. But inside you are full of pretense and rebellion.
(Matthew 23:25-28)

I'm a bit weird when it comes to washing dishes. I rinse
everything before placing it in the dishwasher, but I insist on
the dishes being *visibly spotless* before I put them through the
wash cycle. I suppose I figure that if I take care of all the stuff
I can see, the dishwasher will take care of the stuff I can't see.

But what if we had no other criteria for a clean dish than
visible cleanliness? Suppose we were to rinse dishes with
cold water only until we didn't see any more food on them.
No hot water, no detergent, no scrubbing. Would they be
clean? Well, we might not experience any problems most
of the time; but when it comes to eating and drinking,
the things you can't see (for example, bacteria) are more
dangerous than many of the things *you can see*.

Would you eat in a restaurant that you knew wasn't
sanitizing its plates and silverware? What about going to a
dentist who didn't sterilize dental instruments?

Consider the common cold. It's perhaps the most widely
experienced sickness known to humanity, and still there's
no real cure for it. We just have to let it run its course. Any
medicines you get at your local pharmacy, at best, cover up
the symptoms of a cold; they don't cure it. You can focus on
the externals all you want; but until you take out the virus
itself, the cold is still calling the shots.

Many times I'm afraid we try to treat our spiritual condition
the same way we treat a cold. We want to be holy, but we

try to make that happen by covering up all of the symptoms instead of dealing with the root of the problem.

In this study, I'll examine what it means to be holy. The Bible doesn't make holiness complicated; but as is the case throughout much of Scripture, there is some tension concerning God's initiative and how it connects with our response. But it's worth navigating the tension to get a better understanding of what holiness is.

When you're done with these four sessions, it's my prayer that you'll feel both challenged and set free by what you've discovered.

1

SET APART
FROM ORDINARY TO EXTRAORDINARY

SCRIPTURE
1 PETER 1:13-25

[13]Therefore, once you have your minds ready for action and you are thinking clearly, place your hope completely on the grace that will be brought to you when Jesus Christ is revealed. [14]Don't be conformed to your former desires, those that shaped you when you were ignorant. But, as obedient children, [15]you must be holy in every aspect of your lives, just as the one who called you is holy. [16]It is written, *You will be holy, because I am holy.*[1] [17]Since you call upon a Father who judges all people according to their actions without favoritism, you should conduct yourselves with reverence during the time of your dwelling in a strange land. [18]Live in this way, knowing that you were not liberated by perishable things like silver or gold from the empty lifestyle you inherited from your

---

1. Leviticus 19:2

ancestors. [19]Instead, you were liberated by the precious blood of Christ, like that of a flawless, spotless lamb. [20]Christ was chosen before the creation of the world, but was only revealed at the end of time. This was done for you, [21]who through Christ are faithful to the God who raised him from the dead and gave him glory. So now, your faith and hope should rest in God.

[22]As you set yourselves apart by your obedience to the truth so that you might have genuine affection for your fellow believers, love each other deeply and earnestly. [23]Do this because you have been given new birth—not from the type of seed that decays but from seed that doesn't. This seed is God's life-giving and enduring word.

[24]Thus,
All human life on the earth is like grass,
and all human glory
is like a flower in a field.
The grass dries up
and its flower falls off,

[25]*but the Lord's word endures forever.*[2]
This is the word that was proclaimed to you as good news.

2. Isaiah 40:6-8

INSIGHT AND IDEAS

Have you seen *Veggie Tales,* the Christian animated series that teaches biblical and moral lessons, using salad bar ingredients for its cast? *Veggie Tales* is designed to appeal primarily to kids; but teenagers and adults like watching the show, too. Big Idea, Inc., the producer of *Veggie Tales,* has sold millions of videos since the late 1990s; and each video ends with the same message: "God made you special, and he loves you very much!"

Like many children's programs of the last few decades, *Veggie Tales* reflects a priority of our culture: cultivating positive self-esteem, especially among young people.

But sooner or later, someone comes along and asks the question, "If everyone is special, then is anyone *truly* special?" Or let's take it a bit further: In light of the competitiveness that's predominant in Western society, when we say that someone is a winner, does that automatically mean that those who *aren't* winners are *losers*?

No one wants to be called a loser—even when he or she is actually losing.

And when we say that someone has been *chosen,* aren't we implying that everyone else *wasn't* chosen?

That's fine if you're in the chosen group, but should it really be a surprise when those who *aren't* chosen show a little resentment? This has been the cause of many religious conflicts over the years, and it continues to be the source of conflict today. *My* group is special; *yours* isn't—end of story. (By the way, that's not really something you want to say if you're trying to win friends and influence people.)

GOD'S PEOPLE AND ALL THE REST

Throughout Scripture, we see comparisons and contrasts between God's people and everyone else. In the New Testament, that sometimes takes the form of "the old self versus the new self," those living by the Spirit and those operating according to their own selfish nature—a.k.a. the flesh. When we become Christians, we quickly discover that we're not supposed to act like we did before our relationship with God; and we certainly shouldn't be acting like the nonbelievers. We're special now. Or we're supposed to be. (Sometimes it takes us a while to read the memo and really let it sink in.)

A friend of mine has two young sons; and he has made it a point to be their parent more than their friend, especially while they're really young. He's a loving father, but he's probably more strict than most parents. When he and his wife were at the hospital last year having their third child, I was in the waiting room with other members of his family. The two boys were also there with their grandmother, and the rest of the people who were waiting were marveling at how well-behaved they were. His grandmother explained that their dad had taught them that they *had* to behave. She told me that when the boys were in a public place and other children were throwing tantrums or misbehaving, they'd *point* at the other kids. They knew that they had to behave because of who their father was, but they didn't yet understand why the other kids weren't required to live under the same rules.

HOLINESS COMES FROM GOD

As Christians, we're called and set apart by God. *We* respond to God's grace; but make no mistake, it's *God* who makes the first move, not us. Christians should be different from the rest of the world—but different in a *good* way. However, any goodness we have in us or love that we show to others isn't ultimately because of who we are but because of *who God is*. The *CEB Bible Dictionary says that* the source of holiness is assigned to God alone. "Holiness is God's quintessential nature, distinguishing God from all beings."[3] Holiness is goodness and light, and it's who God is. But as human beings in a broken world, we struggle to comprehend what holiness is without looking through a lens of negativity. To us, goodness means the absence of evil. Light means the absence of darkness. But the reality is, evil is the absence of anything good. Darkness is the absence of light. Goodness and light are real; evil and darkness are what happen when those things aren't present. So since God is the source of holiness, when we reject God or rebel against God, that's when evil and darkness abound.

LIBERATED BY THE BLOOD OF CHRIST

Before we're set apart, God *sets us free* from sin and death. But that's possible only because of Christ. Peter tells us,

---

3. From *Bible Dictionary: The Common English Bible,* (Abingdon Press, 2011); page 174.

"You were not liberated by perishable things like silver or gold from the empty lifestyle you inherited from your ancestors. Instead, you were liberated by the precious blood of Christ, like that of a flawless, spotless lamb" (1 Peter 1:18b-19).

According to the CEB Study Bible, "Peter wants his audience to think about the Passover lamb from Exodus 12. The blood of the Christ is the basis for liberation of believers, just as the blood of the Passover lamb was associated with Israel's liberation from slavery in Egypt."[4] Christ was chosen before the creation of the world to set us free so that we could be set apart. Jesus is holy; and because of our relationship with him, so are we. That makes us different from everyone on the planet who doesn't know Christ.

But because it's something we didn't earn, we must bear in mind that our status is because of God, not because of us. No need to get full of ourselves. Holiness always starts with God; don't go try to make your own.

YOU MUST BE HOLY

Someone once told me that the two things that change you the most are the people you hang out with and the books you read. If this is true, then Christians who spend time talking to God and reading their Bible ought to be the most transformed people on earth. But like many things, this takes some effort. We're holy because God has said so. "But you are a chosen race, a royal priesthood, a holy nation, a

---

4. From "1 Peter," by Jeannine K. Brown, in The Common English Bible Study Bible, edited by Joel B. Green (Common English Bible, 2013); "1 Peter 1:19"; page 464 NT.

people who are God's own possession. You have become this people so that you may speak of the wonderful acts of the one who called you out of darkness into his amazing light" (1 Peter 2:9). But just one chapter before this, Peter says, "You must be holy in every aspect of your lives, just as the one who called you is holy" (1 Peter 1:15). This brings us to one of the big paradoxes of the Christian faith. We're *already holy*, yet we still need to *be holy*. Peter refers to Leviticus 19:2 here as well, "*You will be holy, because I am holy*" (1 Peter 1:16).

It's impossible to live in communion with God, read and hear God's Word on a regular basis and have the Holy Spirit dwell within us and still be the same people we were before all that happened. Sure, we were called holy on day one. But now we must make it our mission to live into that declaration.

SETTING YOURSELF APART

God has set us apart; but we must constantly set ourselves apart, too. Peter says we do that by our "obedience to the truth" (1 Peter 1:22). This doesn't mean that we consider ourselves better than nonbelievers, but it does mean that we're in a much better place than we would be if we didn't know Christ. "Don't be conformed to your former desires, those that shaped you when you were ignorant" (1 Peter 1:14a).

On one hand, we're happy that we've found the Truth; and we want to share him with others. But on the other hand, we know that those to whom we offer Christ are really *us* before we heard and responded to the Good News ourselves. We behave differently from the world not to shame them or condemn them but to show them that there's a better way. We're not ordinary; we're *extraordinary*—because *God* is extraordinary.

As Christians, we believe that there's only one God. But throughout history, even the gods we made up and the evil beings masquerading as gods were never holy. They never *tried* to be. Holiness comes from God alone, and that's why we can't be ordinary anymore once we've had a real God encounter. And the more we encounter God and obey God, the more we set ourselves apart.

'REGULAR' PEOPLE

I grew up watching *The Cosby Show.* In the pilot episode, Bill Cosby's character, Cliff Huxtable, is talking to his son, Theo, about Theo's less-than-stellar grades in school. Theo tells his dad, "You're a doctor and Mom's a lawyer, and you're both successful and everything—and that's great! But maybe *I* was born to be a *regular* person and have a *regular* life. If you weren't a doctor, I wouldn't love you less, because you're my dad. And so, instead of acting disappointed because I'm not like you, maybe you should accept who I am and love me anyway—because I'm your son."

After applause from the audience, Cliff replies, "Theo, that's the *dumbest* thing I've ever heard in my life! No wonder you get D's in everything!"

20

Translation: You're not going to be a "regular person," *because you're my son.* Everyone else's son may be ordinary, but you're going to be *extraordinary.*

The Cosby Show would go on for eight seasons; and during those years, we would learn enough about the Cliff and Clair Huxtable characters to know that even if Theo hadn't buckled down and gotten better grades, Cliff and Clair *did* accept him for who he was and they *would* have loved him anyway—because he was their son. (Incidentally, Theo went on to get a psychology degree from New York University.)

In the same way, holiness should never become a performance issue. Otherwise, God becomes a tyrant—the demanding father who is never satisfied, even when we've done our best.

Get this much straight: We're accepted by God because of what Jesus did on the cross, *period.* But we have such riches in Christ that God no doubt has high expectations and hopes for us. Living in bondage to sin the way the rest of the world does is simply not an option.

So how do we respond to a God who expects us to be holy in every aspect of our lives? Is this even doable? I'm from the school of thought that says that God doesn't usually ask the impossible of us but that when God does ask it, there's *always* a provision to help us do the impossible. We have the Holy Spirit dwelling within us, who, under normal circumstances, should be regularly filling us. That's huge.

READY FOR ACTION

More clues for how to tackle holiness can be found in 1 Peter 1:13: "Therefore, once you have your minds ready for action and you are thinking clearly, place your hope completely on the grace that will be brought to you when Jesus Christ is revealed." A big part of the quest for holiness happens in our mind. We use our mind to talk ourselves into things *and* out of things. We weigh options with our mind and make decisions with our mind. Our intellect, emotions, and will are all connected with our mind. So if we can figure out how to use our mind correctly, the rest of our pursuit of holiness is that much easier.

Peter tells us that our mind should to be trained to always be ready for action. And we must learn to think clearly and have sense enough to avoid certain situations when we're *not* thinking clearly. And we mustn't forget hope. Essentially, we must learn to hang on to the good and let go of the bad. Often, that means learning how to think differently; and that takes discipline. (We'll deal with discipline in the next session.)

Bob the Tomato and Larry the Cucumber were right: "God made [us] special, and he loves [us] very much." We learn this when we're kids; but as we mature in Christ, we realize that this comes with some responsibilities. We simply can't be who we really are and act like everyone else—not for long anyway, not if we're going to have real peace.

There's a reason for that: We've been set apart.

QUESTIONS

1. How do we get our mind ready for action? How do we know when we're not thinking clearly (1 Peter 1:13)?

2. How do our desires shape us? How do we change our desires (1 Peter 1:14)?

3. How do we make every aspect of our lives holy? Describe a scenario where a person is being holy only in *some* aspects of his or her life. What are the potential outcomes (1 Peter 1:15)?

4. Why does God expect Christians to be holy (1 Peter 1:16)?

5. What is the connection between holiness and the blood of Christ (1 Peter 1:19)?

6. What happens when our faith and hope aren't resting in God (1 Peter 1:21)?

7. What does it mean to set ourselves apart? How does setting ourselves apart relate to God's setting us apart (1 Peter 1:22)?

8. What is the new birth Peter mentions in 1 Peter 1:23? How do we know whether we've experienced this new birth?

9. Who are God's people today? Why might this be considered a controversial question?

10. Is it possible to be a Christian and *not* pursue holiness? Why, or why not?

2

CELEBRATION OF WHAT?
'DISCIPLINE' ISN'T A FOUR-LETTER WORD

SCRIPTURE
HEBREWS 12:1-17

[1]So then let's also run the race that is laid out in front of us,
since we have such a great cloud of witnesses surrounding us.
Let's throw off any extra baggage, get rid of the sin that trips us
up, [2]and fix our eyes on Jesus, faith's pioneer and perfecter. He
endured the cross, ignoring the shame, for the sake of the joy
that was laid out in front of him, and sat down at the right side of
God's throne.

[3]Think about the one who endured such opposition from sinners
so that you won't be discouraged and you won't give up. [4]In
your struggle against sin, you haven't resisted yet to the point
of shedding blood, [5]and you have forgotten the encouragement
that addresses you as sons and daughters:

My child, don't make light of the Lord's discipline

or give up when you are corrected by him,

⁶because the Lord disciplines whomever he loves,

and he punishes every son or daughter whom he accepts.[1]

⁷Bear hardship for the sake of discipline. God is treating you like sons and daughters! What child isn't disciplined by his or her father? ⁸But if you don't experience discipline, which happens to all children, then you are illegitimate and not real sons and daughters. ⁹What's more, we had human parents who disciplined us, and we respected them for it. How much more should we submit to the Father of spirits and live? ¹⁰Our human parents disciplined us for a little while, as it seemed best to them, but God does it for our benefit so that we can share his holiness. ¹¹No discipline is fun while it lasts, but it seems painful at the time. Later, however, it yields the peaceful fruit of righteousness for those who have been trained by it.

¹²So strengthen your drooping hands and weak knees! ¹³Make straight paths for your feet so that if any part is lame, it will be healed rather than injured more seriously. ¹⁴Pursue the goal of peace along with everyone—and holiness as well, because no one will see the Lord without it. ¹⁵Make sure that no one misses out on God's grace. Make sure that no root of bitterness grows up that might cause trouble and pollute many people. ¹⁶Make sure that no one becomes sexually immoral or ungodly like Esau. He

---

1. Proverbs 3:11-12

sold his inheritance as the oldest son for one meal. [17]You know that afterward, when he wanted to inherit the blessing, he was rejected because he couldn't find a way to change his heart and life, though he looked for it with tears.

INSIGHT AND IDEAS

If you visit a McDonald's or similar community gathering place on a weekday morning and listen in on some of the conversations among the regular patrons, you'll hear all kinds of talk about politics and the news of the day. And if you ask someone who's Baby Boomer age or older what's wrong with society today, you might just hear the D-word:

"Parents don't discipline their kids anymore."

"People don't understand self-discipline."

"They should bring back the draft so that the younger generation can learn discipline."

There are probably many people out there who don't think of positive things when they hear *discipline*. The word has a number of different meanings, but there's a common connection between all of them. For the verb *discipline,* Google Dictionary lists three main definitions:

1. train (someone) to obey rules or a code of behavior, using punishment to correct disobedience.

2. punish or rebuke (someone) formally for an offense.

27

3. train oneself to do something in a controlled and
habitual way.

Discipline comes from Middle English by way of Old French,
derived from Latin; and it's connected with the concept of
instruction and knowledge. *Disciple* is closely related to the
word *discipline,* as might be suspected if one notes the root
both words share.

But impressive etymologies and entertaining factoids aside,
most of us don't really enjoy discipline. The Bible explicitly
concurs with this observation when it says, "No discipline
is fun while it lasts, but it seems painful at the time"
(Hebrews 12:11a).

So why on earth would anyone *voluntarily* put himself or
herself through discipline?

Because the results are worth it. Discipline is like an
investment, and the Bible is clear that this investment brings
a substantial payoff: "Later, however, [discipline] yields the
peaceful fruit of righteousness for those who have been
trained by it" (Hebrews 12:11b).

PARENTS JUST DON'T UNDERSTAND, OR DO THEY?

Discipline starts when we're small children; and for most
of us, it's provided by our parent(s). We have very little say
in the matter. And when I look back on my childhood and
teenage years, I believe that's a good thing.

If my mom hadn't been calling the shots when I was a kid, I never would have . . .

  . . . gone to bed before midnight.

  . . . stopped at just one bowl of ice cream.

  . . . cleaned my room.

  . . . gone to school when I didn't feel like doing so.

  . . . eaten anything green.

  . . . interacted with people I didn't like.

  . . . turned off the TV set.

  . . . behaved at school. (OK, I didn't do this anyway.)

Suppose I had been able to do whatever I'd wanted to do when I was growing up. I probably would've never made it to college, and I doubt that I'd be able to survive in the workplace today. You see, our parents disciplined us when we were young because we didn't have the ability (or the desire) to discipline ourselves. But as we got older, this responsibility fell on us; and the habits we learned as kids stuck with us. That's what the Bible is getting at when it says, "Train children in the way they should go; when they grow old, they won't depart from it" (Proverbs 22:6).

Of course, many of us do "depart from it" for a season. But if a foundation of discipline has been properly laid, as we mature, we usually get ourselves back on track. Once we're on our own, we must rely on ourselves, God, our spouse (if applicable), and others to provide discipline. And it's on a voluntary basis; because, ultimately, we can do whatever we want when we're adults, which means that submitting to discipline is an ongoing act of will.

THROWING OFF THE BAGGAGE

One reason we discipline ourselves is so that we can live better lives. The author of Hebrews refers to our life of faith as a race: "So then let's also run the race that is laid out in front of us, since we have such a great cloud of witnesses surrounding us. Let's throw off any extra baggage, get rid of the sin that trips us up" (Hebrews 12:1).

I work in the publishing industry; and a significant part of my day is spent online, so I'm very dependent on technology. I have desktop computers at home and at work, a laptop, a smartphone, and a tablet. I like to be connected wherever I go.

Since I obviously don't have enough gadgets, I recently bought a Google Chromebook. A Chromebook is like a regular laptop, with a few significant differences. It's lighter, thinner, faster, has a longer battery life, and doesn't run software. It doesn't use Windows or Apple's OS operating system; it uses Google Chrome OS. Files aren't generally stored on the laptop itself but "in the cloud," which means that files are accessible from any machine with an Internet connection. Chromebooks can't get viruses, and they don't slow down over time like many other computers tend to do.

My Chromebook is the least expensive piece of technology I have, but I enjoy using it more than any other computer I own. Why? There's no baggage, nothing to slow it down. It's easy to use, and it does 90–95 percent of what I need a computer to do on a daily basis. I can use it virtually anywhere, and I never have to wait for anything. I can focus on what I need to focus on because there are fewer distractions such as software updates and antivirus updates to sidetrack me. My Chromebook's simplicity makes it more effective and helps me get more work done.

Life works the same way. How much more could we accomplish for the kingdom of God if we didn't complicate our lives with so many useless things that slow us down?

This is where the race metaphor really hits home. A serious runner wears the lightest, most wind-resistant clothing possible. And he or she watches where he or she is running to avoid rocks and other potential hazards. Can you imagine a competitive runner wearing a heavy backpack or bringing luggage along on a race?

Of course not, but many of us don't think twice about running the race of faith with baggage. Whether it's garbage from earlier in our lives that we never properly dealt with, foolish financial decisions we make like living beyond our means, acquiring too much stuff we don't need, or worrying about problems we have no control over, most of us could stand a life-simplification makeover to help us focus on what really matters.

THE DEVIL AND ME

If holiness involves purging sin from our lives and becoming more like Jesus Christ, then part of getting rid of sin involves getting rid of *opportunities* to sin. Paul said it succinctly: "Don't provide an opportunity for the devil" (Ephesians 4:27). If a person, place, or thing is going to tempt us to sin in some way, doesn't it make sense to minimize our exposure to it if possible? But we often don't do this because we're either foolish or in denial about our own weaknesses and our love of sin.

A wise, mature believer learns to outwit not only evil but also himself. My new self, for example, regularly strategizes against my old self. I have to, because the old Shane is constantly trying to resurrect himself even though he has been put to death. (See Galatians 2:20 if that statement has you scratching your head.) I know my strengths and my weaknesses. And with the exception of God, I know myself better than anyone else knows me. When I use that intelligence to make good decisions, it's both a sign of maturity and an act of discipline. And if I continue to do this, I'll see a significant amount of good fruit in my life.

PRACTICING SPIRITUAL DISCIPLINES

This brings me to the subject of spiritual disciplines, such as praying, reading the Bible, and fasting. At first, the way the word *discipline* is used here may seem different from the way I've been using it; but it's really the same thing. It all comes back to the concept of training ourselves.

But spiritual disciplines can be difficult to practice. For example, the most powerful prayer times and Bible study sessions I've ever had usually started with me pulling myself away, kicking and screaming, from everything else and starting with what seemed like a desert experience.

The first few minutes of prayer and Bible study are never easy for me, and I can find plenty of distractions to pull me away without even trying hard. But when I stick with it, I'm rarely disappointed; and I see results.

It's a lot like running. I've never liked running. I don't like being out of breath, I don't like pains in my side, and I can't stand how time slows to a standstill when I'm using a stopwatch to track my progress. But I love the results I get from running. I feel and look better, and I have more endurance during other athletic activities. Plus, I have more energy in general. (After a few minutes, running even gets easier, once I get through the "I want to give up on this and go to Dunkin' Donuts" stage.) Getting results from spiritual disciplines requires similar perseverance.

The Word of God cleanses us and transforms us through the renewing of our mind. So if we're serious about pursuing holiness, then spending time listening to God through prayer and reading Scripture is key. But we should never wait until we feel like doing it before we actually start doing it. Right feelings follow right actions; it hardly ever happens the other way around. Remember, "no discipline [even self-discipline] is fun while it lasts."

WHEN GOD INTERVENES

If we don't discipline ourselves, many times God will step in and do it for us. God loves us but is more than willing to make us uncomfortable for a time if it's going to benefit us long term.

This reminds me of my many experiences visiting the dentist. Because I wasn't as disciplined as I should have been with oral hygiene in my teens and twenties, I've been forced to give dentists a lot more of my money over the years than I would have otherwise. And the pain of forking over all that cash was just the tip of the iceberg. I've also spent countless hours in chairs, getting fillings, crowns—even a couple of root canals along the way. I would have spared myself much of that pain if only I'd eaten fewer sweets and flossed more regularly a few years ago. So after spending thousands of dollars, wisdom has taught me to take better care of my teeth now. I'm not sure I'd have figured that out without experiencing some pain along the way. But if I'd avoided the pain that came with crowns and root canals, imagine how much worse my pain might have been!

When it comes to our lives, God sees the big picture, and would probably rather that we go through a little pain now than a lot of pain later. What's unfortunate for us is that God doesn't usually feel the need to fill us in on all the details along the way. So if we don't understand the concept of discipline, we might think that God has abandoned us or that we're facing spiritual attack.

A few years ago, a pastor told me about a bad week he'd had: "I think my family is under spiritual attack," he said.

"What makes you say that?" I asked.

"Well, two days ago I got a speeding ticket. Yesterday my son got one, too. And this morning my wife was stopped for speeding and received a ticket, as well."

"I don't think you're being attacked," I said.

"You don't?"

"No, if anything, God is trying to tell you and your family that you need to slow down!"

Part of discipline is facing consequences for our actions so that we don't make the same mistakes—or even worse mistakes—in the future.

PURSUING HOLINESS

The writer of Hebrews tells us to "pursue holiness" (Hebrews 12:14) and adds a sobering consequence for those who don't: "No one will see the Lord without it." There are at least a couple of principles I can draw from this verse. First, holiness doesn't chase us down or smack us in the face; we have to pursue it. Remember the paradox from Chapter 1: We've already been made holy by Christ's death on the cross, but we're also instructed to be holy. This means that being holy is something we do actively, not passively. Second, we can't pursue God and pursue sin at the same time. Nineteenth-century Methodist theologian Adam Clarke had this to say about Hebrews 12:14:

> [Holiness is] that state of continual sanctification, that life of purity and detachment from the world and all its lusts, without which

detachment and sanctity no man shall see the Lord—shall never enjoy his presence in the world of blessedness. To see God, in the Hebrew phrase, is to enjoy him; and without holiness of heart and life this is impossible. No soul can be fit for heaven that has not suitable dispositions for the place.[2]

Let's recap. To really experience God, we must pursue holiness. This requires self-discipline, which involves throwing off excess baggage and avoiding the sin that waits to trip us up.

All of this, of course, is easier said than done. Besides our own selfish desires and the spiritual adversaries we must deal with, there's a whole world out there that's not exactly trying to make it easier for us to become more Christlike. I'll break that down a bit in the next chapter.

---

2. From "Commentary on Hebrews 12:14," in *Adam Clarke's Commentary on the Bible,* by Adam Clarke, (Thomas Nelson, 1997) *http://www.studylight.org/com/acc/view. cgi?bk=57&ch=12.* Accessed 22 February 2014.

QUESTIONS

1. What is "the race that is laid out in front of us" (Hebrews 12:1)? How do we win this race?

2. Who are the cloud of witnesses that surround us (Hebrews 12:1)? Why does the author of Hebrews connect them with the race we're running?

3. How is Jesus faith's pioneer and perfecter (Hebrews 12:2)?

4. Why should we find it comforting when we're being disciplined by God (Hebrews 12:5-7)?

5. What is the peaceful fruit of righteousness that comes from discipline (Hebrews 12:11)?

6. What does it mean to make straight paths for our feet? How do we do this (Hebrews 12:13)?

7. Why is it important to pursue holiness (Hebrews 12:14)?

8. What does it mean to "see the Lord" (Hebrews 12:14)?

9. What is the connection between discipline and God's grace (Hebrews 12:15)?

10. Why does the author of Hebrews specifically mention sexual immorality in Hebrews 12:16?

11. What are the implications for repentance in Hebrews 12:17? Is it possible to want to repent but not be able to do so? Why, or why not?

3

CHRISTIAN MEETS WORLD
STAYING CLEAN IN HOSTILE TERRITORY

SCRIPTURE
JOHN 17:1-23

[1]When Jesus finished saying these things, he looked up to heaven and said, "Father, the time has come. Glorify your Son, so that the Son can glorify you. [2]You gave him authority over everyone so that he could give eternal life to everyone you gave him. [3]This is eternal life: to know you, the only true God, and Jesus Christ whom you sent. [4]I have glorified you on earth by finishing the work you gave me to do. [5]Now, Father, glorify me in your presence with the glory I shared with you before the world was created.

[6]"I have revealed your name to the people you gave me from this world. They were yours and you gave them to me, and they have kept your word. [7]Now they know that everything you have given me comes from you. [8]This is because I gave them the words that

you gave me, and they received them. They truly understood that I came from you, and they believed that you sent me.

[9]"I'm praying for them. I'm not praying for the world but for those you gave me, because they are yours. [10]Everything that is mine is yours and everything that is yours is mine; I have been glorified in them. [11]I'm no longer in the world, but they are in the world, even as I'm coming to you. Holy Father, watch over them in your name, the name you gave me, that they will be one just as we are one. [12]When I was with them, I watched over them in your name, the name you gave to me, and I kept them safe. None of them were lost, except the one who was destined for destruction, so that scripture would be fulfilled. [13]Now I'm coming to you and I say these things while I'm in the world so that they can share completely in my joy. [14]I gave your word to them and the world hated them, because they don't belong to this world, just as I don't belong to this world. [15]I'm not asking that you take them out of this world but that you keep them safe from the evil one. [16]They don't belong to this world, just as I don't belong to this world. [17]Make them holy in the truth; your word is truth. [18]As you sent me into the world, so I have sent them into the world. [19]I made myself holy on their behalf so that they also would be made holy in the truth.

[20]"I'm not praying only for them but also for those who believe in me because of their word. [21]I pray they will be one, Father, just as you are in me and I am in you. I pray that they also will be in us,

so that the world will believe that you sent me. ²²I've given them the glory that you gave me so that they can be one just as we are one. ²³I'm in them and you are in me so that they will be made perfectly one. Then the world will know that you sent me and that you have loved them just as you loved me.

INSIGHT AND IDEAS

I live in downtown Nashville not far from Bridgestone Arena, a multi-purpose facility where the Country Music Association Awards are held each year, and where many A-list music artists perform concerts. Last September, country-pop crossover artist Taylor Swift brought her *Red Tour* to the arena, and swarms of teen and preteen girls (and their parents) descended on the downtown area to see the show. Huge trucks with tour branding lined the adjacent streets, and radio station tents and souvenir booths out front were overflowing with people a couple of hours before the show. I was passing by when I noticed something in the middle of all the festivities that stuck out like a sore thumb.

Just outside the arena, at the corner of Fifth and Broadway, was a group of people holding inflammatory placards that proclaimed hellfire and damnation for all who were coming to watch the concert that evening. (To be fair, they were probably judging the tourists entering the nearby honky-tonks too.) I was embarrassed and a little angry. How could people who called themselves Christians come across as so mean and judgmental? I briefly considered initiating an exchange with the group, but wisdom quickly prevailed and I kept walking. I'd been down that road before, and it had never ended well.

So instead, I did what any conscientious twenty-first-century Christian activist wanting to make a difference would do: I tweeted my disapproval and posted a photo on Instagram. That showed 'em!

I'm sure that I wasn't the only person passing by that evening who didn't want Christianity associated with the people protesting out front. Don't get me wrong, I'm certainly not defending most of our culture's popular music. There are many songs on the radio with unwholesome lyrics—and these are the edited versions. If I were a parent, I'd keep my kids away from all of it as long as possible. But I'm pretty certain that completely withdrawing from the culture and condemning it isn't the most effective approach.

CHRISTIANS AND CULTURE

Fringe groups aside, even mainstream Christians are divided on how much culture accommodation is too much. On one end of the spectrum there are those who try to avoid anything that even resembles popular culture. They attempt to shield themselves and their families from everything perceived to be "secular." There's even a subgroup within this group that takes cues from cultural styles but translates them to an alternate universe where everything is "Christian." Then there are those Christians who seem to embrace everything the entertainment industry cranks out, no questions asked. Some are nominal Christians to be sure, but others are committed believers who sincerely feel they won't be adversely affected by explicit language or graphic imagery. Then there are those who try to play it down the middle— which doesn't always produce the desired results.

About ten years ago, when I was a church youth worker, the youth minister and I were planning a lock-in event, and we decided to use a current film that went well with the message we were preaching. The only problem with our plan was the movie was rated R for language. No sex scenes or graphic violence—just some bad words. What would we do? I came up with what I thought was a foolproof plan.

About that time, an entrepreneurial company was hawking a new gadget in Christian bookstores that would supposedly bleep out swear words from movies and television shows, making them more acceptable to Christian families. I talked to people who said that they'd tried it; and they assured me, "It's great!" The technology worked with closed-captions, and I figured that it was the perfect solution to our dilemma. Christian bookstores couldn't keep this gadget in stock, I discovered; so I was *sure* that it would do all it claimed. What could possibly go wrong?

I shouldn't have asked. To make a long story short, we had apparently picked the one movie from my lifetime that had been released to DVD without closed captions. (I'm sure there

43

have been others; but TV shows have been closed-captioned since the 1970s, for crying out loud. I thought that everything was closed-captioned.) So we stopped the movie two minutes in because of all the F-bombs. Then we awkwardly suggested that everyone play games and help themselves to more food. The one consolation I had was that the senior pastor, who was "too old to pull all-nighters," had already gone home, so he managed to miss our little cinematic debacle.

AVOIDING THE 'CHRISTIAN BUBBLE'

This incident illustrates the balancing act Christians face as we try to be *in* the world, but not *of* it. In the same way that Jesus was sent into the world for others, those of us who believe in him are sent into the world, not for our own sake but for those who will hear the gospel through us. The danger, of course, is that rather than being salt and light, we risk being caught up in the very stuff we've been saved from. And that's why some Christians isolate themselves or establish their domain inside the "Christian bubble."

The prayer Jesus prays in John 17, however, gives us some clues that withdrawing from the world is not the optimal choice for Christians who are serious about building God's kingdom. Referring to the disciples, Jesus says this: "I'm praying for them. I'm not praying for the world but for those you gave me, because they are yours" (John 17:9).

What an odd statement! After all, didn't Jesus become human and come to earth because "God so loved the world" (John 3:16)? Yet instead of praying for the whole world, Jesus prays for a ragtag group of followers. Being the Son of God and all, you'd think he'd pray big; but at this particular moment, he appears to pray small.

That tells me that a lot must've been riding on this little band of believers. Jesus confirms this as he broadens the scope of his prayer later: "I'm not praying only for them but also for those who believe in me because of their word" (John 17:20).

If you're a Christian, that includes you. But you probably didn't become a Christian because of a direct message or a supernatural visitation from God. Chances are, you heard about Jesus from a friend, pastor, or family member. Maybe you read a book by a Christian author or heard the gospel when you were a kid in vacation Bible school. However you got the message, it most likely came through another believer. And that's the point. Jesus didn't save us to spend the rest of our lives in an exclusive Christian club. There's work to be done sharing the gospel and making disciples, but we have to do it out in the world because most of the world probably isn't going to come to us.

Paul wrote a clarification in 1 Corinthians that seems to confirm this very idea:

> I wrote to you in my earlier letter not to associate with sexually immoral people. But I wasn't talking about the sexually immoral people in the outside world by any means—or the greedy, or the swindlers, or people who worship false gods—otherwise, you would have to leave the world entirely! (1 Corinthians 5:9-10)

45

Boom! Note that Paul wasn't saying that it was OK for Christians to worship false gods, be sexually immoral, greedy, or swindle others. But hanging out with those who claimed to be Christians but compromised in these ways *was* off limits. Perhaps this had a connection with the Christian unity that Jesus prayed for in John 17. How can believers who are supposedly unified work to build opposing kingdoms?

Plus, in our pursuit of holiness, we face opposition from spiritual forces, the world, and even our own flesh. Perhaps Paul was asserting that the church is the one place we should be able to find accountability and be built up instead of being torn down.

GETTING OUR FEET DIRTY

If we're doing what God has called us to do to reach the lost, we're going to be exposed to things that make us uncomfortable and even "pollute" us. This doesn't mean that we've sinned, although the enemy would like nothing better than to use these things as possible entry points into our lives so we *will* sin. This is where we must actively "be holy" or else we make ourselves vulnerable.

This makes me think of Jesus' washing the disciples' feet:

> Jesus and his disciples were sharing the evening meal. The devil had already provoked Judas, Simon Iscariot's son, to betray Jesus. Jesus knew the Father had given everything into his hands and that he had come from God and was returning to God. So he got up from the table and took off his robes. Picking up a

linen towel, he tied it around his waist. Then he poured water into a washbasin and began to wash the disciples' feet, drying them with the towel he was wearing. When Jesus came to Simon Peter, Peter said to him, "Lord, are you going to wash my feet?"

Jesus replied, "You don't understand what I'm doing now, but you will understand later."

"No!" Peter said. "You will never wash my feet!"

Jesus replied, "Unless I wash you, you won't have a place with me."

Simon Peter said, "Lord, not only my feet but also my hands and my head!"

Jesus responded, "Those who have bathed need only to have their feet washed, because they are completely clean. (John 13:2-10a)

John Wesley said that washing one's feet meant "walking holy and undefiled." Methodist theologian Adam Clarke was less certain about the meaning of these verses, but did share a popular point-of-view:

If these last words of our Lord had any spiritual reference, it is not easy to say what it was. A common opinion is the following: He who is washed—who is justified through the blood of the Lamb, needeth only to wash his feet—to regulate all his affections and desires; and to get, by faith, his conscience cleansed from any fresh guilt, which he may have contracted since his justification.[1]

---

1. From "Commentary on John 13:10," in *Adam Clarke's Commentary on the Bible,* by Adam Clarke, (Thomas Nelson, 1997) *http://www.studylight.org/com/acc/view.cgi?bk=42&ch=13.* Accessed 23 February 2014.

Put another way, getting your feet dirty doesn't make you *truly* dirty. People in biblical culture presumably bathed before they shared an important meal or attended a function; and since there were no freeways, pavement, and sidewalks back in the day, their feet would get dirty en route to their destination and would have to be washed. But biblical people didn't have to bathe again, because their bath was still "in effect," if you will.

Jesus understood better than anyone the dangers we face and the risks we take when we go into the world to reach the lost. That's why he prayed:

> I'm not asking that you take them out of this world but that you keep them safe from the evil one. They don't belong to this world, just as I don't belong to this world. Make them holy in the truth; your word is truth. As you sent me into the world, so I have sent them into the world. I made myself holy on their behalf so that they also would be made holy in the truth. (John 17:15-19)

Just as Jesus was set apart, we're set apart. He's the one who makes us holy so that we can confidently go into the world and do the things he did.

But the idea of pursuing holiness raises some questions: Do we ever really arrive? When are we fully mature? Can Christians reach perfection in this life? We'll explore this concept in the last chapter.

QUESTIONS

1. What is the eternal life Jesus mentions in John 17:2-3?

2. What does it mean to be glorified? How has Christ been glorified?

3. Why didn't Jesus pray for the world in John 17:9?

4. Jesus prayed that believers would become one. Has this prayer been realized? Why, or why not?

5. What did Jesus mean when he said that "the world hated them" (John 17:14)? In what ways does the world today hate believers? How should Christians respond?

6. How did Jesus make himself holy on our behalf? What does it mean to be holy in the truth (John 17:19)?

7. What does Jesus predict in John 17:20? How does this relate to Christians today?

8. What is the glory that Jesus has given us (John 17:22)?

9. Are there times when it is appropriate for Christians to retreat from the world? If so, when?

4

NOT YET PERFECT
PURSUING GOD'S UPWARD CALL

SCRIPTURE
PHILIPPIANS 3:1-16

[1]So then, my brothers and sisters, be glad in the Lord. It's no trouble for me to repeat the same things to you because they will help keep you on track. [2]Watch out for the "dogs." Watch out for people who do evil things. Watch out for those who insist on circumcision, which is really mutilation. [3]We are the circumcision. We are the ones who serve by God's Spirit and who boast in Christ Jesus. We don't put our confidence in rituals performed on the body, [4]though I have good reason to have this kind of confidence. If anyone else has reason to put their confidence in physical advantages, I have even more:

[5]I was circumcised on the eighth day.
I am from the people of Israel and the tribe of Benjamin.
I am a Hebrew of the Hebrews.

With respect to observing the Law, I'm a Pharisee.

[6]With respect to devotion to the faith, I harassed the church.

With respect to righteousness under the Law, I'm blameless.

[7]These things were my assets, but I wrote them off as a loss for the sake of Christ. [8]But even beyond that, I consider everything a loss in comparison with the superior value of knowing Christ Jesus my Lord. I have lost everything for him, but what I lost I think of as sewer trash, so that I might gain Christ [9]and be found in him. In Christ I have a righteousness that is not my own and that does not come from the Law but rather from the faithfulness of Christ. It is the righteousness of God that is based on faith. [10]The righteousness that I have comes from knowing Christ, the power of his resurrection, and the participation in his sufferings. It includes being conformed to his death [11]so that I may perhaps reach the goal of the resurrection of the dead.

[12]It's not that I have already reached this goal or have already been perfected, but I pursue it, so that I may grab hold of it because Christ grabbed hold of me for just this purpose. [13]Brothers and sisters, I myself don't think I've reached it, but I do this one thing: I forget about the things behind me and reach out for the things ahead of me. [14]The goal I pursue is the prize of God's upward call in Christ Jesus. [15]So all of us who are spiritually mature should think this way, and if anyone thinks differently, God will reveal it to him or her. [16]Only let's live in a way that is consistent with whatever level we have reached.

INSIGHT AND IDEAS

If anything illustrates the intensity and magnitude surrounding the concept of trying to be perfect, it's the modern day Olympic Games. Each even-numbered year, young athletes from around the world come together to compete against one another in hope of winning a gold medal—some in time-based events, where the fastest athlete wins, and others in competitions that are judged and scored based on how well they complete a routine.

The second category has always fascinated me, partly because the possibility of an athlete spending years training full time, only to have everything fall apart in a split second is a very real one. There's only one gold medal for each event; and while an athlete would rather receive a silver or bronze medal than none at all, no one truly invests so many years of his or her life just to come in second or third. Everyone shows up for the gold. And to get the gold, an athlete has to be *perfect*—or at least be the one closest to perfect in the competition.

But in some sports, even perfection is a moving target.

I was 11 years old when American gymnast Mary Lou Retton won five medals in the 1984 Summer Olympics, including the gold in the individual all-around women's gymnastics competition. At the time, she was the best in the world. But suppose that time travel were possible, and we could bring 16-year-old Mary Lou Retton from 1984 into the present day to compete against today's top female gymnasts. What would happen? She wouldn't even qualify, because the sport has progressed and the routines have changed. "Perfect" in 1984 wouldn't cut it today.

HOLINESS ISN'T ABOUT KEEPING SCORE

Sometimes we think of holiness as an Olympic event and of sin as those mistakes and imperfections that deduct points from our score. We understand from Romans 3:23 that "all have sinned and fall short of God's glory," so we know that no one's getting a perfect score. We may even know enough about theology to understand that Jesus is the only one to have scored a ten. And if we have an understanding of imputed, or ascribed, righteousness, we know that Jesus' perfect score has been assigned to us, even though we don't deserve it.

But at this point, we tend to fall into one of two equal, opposite errors. The first is legalism, or performance-based Christianity. We try to "earn" the perfect ten that we already have (and fail miserably). The other is an apathetic cheap grace theology that says if I accept Jesus as Savior, I don't have to change my behavior or do anything else. In other words, Jesus got a ten, so there's no need for me to even show up to the event now. Old school theologians call this *antinomianism*.

A big problem with both of these views, especially legalism, is that they're focused on externals, not internals. Instead of being passionate about pursuing Christ and becoming as much like him as we can, we get caught up with keeping score. Or we become slackers. Either way, the results aren't pretty.

If you've played many games of pick-up basketball, you know that there are at least three types of people playing. First there's the super-competitive player. This person calls fouls where most people would overlook them, becomes easily frustrated, pushes himself or herself to the limit, and knows the precise score at all times. Mistakes are unacceptable—it's as if the fate of the world is riding on this game.

Then there's the person who barely shows up, is never fully engaged, loses interest quickly, and wouldn't play defense if his life depended on it. He doesn't know the score of the game, and rarely ever asks anyone else what it is. (As you might expect, people in the second group really tend to frustrate those in the first group—and vice versa.)

Finally there's the third person—the one who's on the court because of a love for playing basketball. This person wants to score as many points, get as many rebounds, and block as many shots as possible; but more than that, she wants to just enjoy playing the game. She'll ask what the score is from time to time; but she's always more focused on starting the next game than obsessing over this one, because she loves the game. It's impossible for her to get enough basketball.

Who among these three would you rather play basketball with? I'd rather play with the one who really loves the game.

CHRISTIAN PERFECTION

John Wesley, the founder of the Methodist movement, taught a controversial doctrine called *Christian perfection.* (You may also see this doctrine referred to from time to time as *entire sanctification* or *perfect love.*) This was arguably Wesley's most misunderstood teaching; and he spent a considerable amount of time defending it, largely against mischaracterizations of it.

The big controversy surrounding Christian perfection centered mostly around the question of whether or not a Christian can reach it in this life; and if so, is it *sinless* perfection? Christian perfection doesn't create as much controversy today; but that probably has a lot to do with the fact that it isn't being taught as much, even among believers who are descendants of the original Methodist movement. Ask most Christians today about the idea of becoming "perfect," and they'll tell you that it's not possible until we reach heaven.

Some are quick to point out that rather than absolute sinless perfection, the word rendered *perfect* in most English translations might be better translated *complete* or *mature.* Others would also add that Christian perfection is more about having God's fullness and showing perfect love than about achieving a state of sinless perfection. I confess that I used to see this as a cop-out by Christians who wanted to take all the meat out of entire sanctification doctrine, making it more palatable to the masses. And perhaps that's the case with some. But once I started understanding sin and holiness in light of something Jesus said in Matthew 22, the connection between perfection and love made much more sense to me:

> When the Pharisees heard that Jesus had left the Sadducees speechless, they met together. One of them, a legal expert, tested him. "Teacher, what is the greatest commandment in the Law?"
>
> He replied, "*You must love the Lord your God with all your heart, with all your being,*[1] *and with all your mind.* This is the first and greatest commandment. And the second is like it: *You must love your neighbor as you love yourself.*[2] All the Law and the Prophets depend on these two commands." (Matthew 22:34-40)

Essentially, we sin when we're not loving God and neighbor. But when we *do* love God and neighbor, we're actualizing the holiness we've already received through Christ's finished work on the cross. Peter made this connection when he wrote, "Above all, show sincere love to each other, because love brings about the forgiveness of many sins" (1 Peter 4:8). This concept is also developed in 1 John:

> This is how love has been perfected in us, so that we can have confidence on the Judgment Day, because we are exactly the same as God is in this world. There is no fear in love, but perfect love drives out fear, because fear expects punishment. The person who is afraid has not been made perfect in love. We love because God first loved us. (1 John 4:17-19)

---

1. Deuteronomy 6:5
2. Leviticus 19:18

When we're focusing on externals, that is, worrying more about the scoreboard than playing a good game, we're operating out of fear. Whether we say that we believe such a thing or not, we're really living our lives as if God is accepting us based on how we perform, not on the basis of Jesus Christ's death on the cross. But the fear of not being good enough is driven out when we focus on experiencing and showing perfect love.

LOVING MORE, SINNING LESS

So rather than ask whether it's possible to eradicate all sin in this life, a better question to ask might be, is it possible to reach a point where we're constantly filled with and showing perfect love? And how do we quantify love anyway? Can I ever reach the point that I'm unable to love God and neighbor more tomorrow than I do today? For me, that point is hard to imagine. Perhaps that's why some Christians speak of perfection as a process or journey ("going on to perfection") rather than a state or destination ("being perfect"). Think of a curve in geometry that approaches a line going to infinity without ever quite touching it. The direction you're traveling on the curve and the fact that you're approaching the line is significantly more important right now than reaching the line or crossing it.

Remember, we don't try to become perfect so that we can be saved; we're saved so that we can become perfect. Paul writes to the Philippians:

> It's not that I have already reached this goal or have already been perfected, but I pursue it, so that I may grab hold of it because Christ grabbed hold of me for just this purpose. Brothers and sisters, I myself don't think I've reached it, but I do this one thing: I forget about the things behind me and reach out for the things ahead of me. The goal I pursue is the prize of God's upward call in Christ Jesus. (Philippians 3:12-14)

Holiness to Paul is about constantly answering God's call to fullness of life in Christ, not focusing on keeping laws and commandments. But as Christians mature and learn to love in a more perfect way, they're naturally going to sin less.

Paul doesn't seem to make this a big point of contention, because he writes: "So all of us who are spiritually mature should think this way, and if anyone thinks differently, God will reveal it to him or her. Only let's live in a way that is consistent with whatever level we have reached" (Philippians 3:15-16). So whether living a holy life is analogous to playing a videogame that can be beaten (think old-school Super Mario Brothers and saving the princess) or one that advances through infinite levels, being holy is not an option for Christians.

'SINLESS PERFECTION'

But the pivotal question for many people remains, can someone reach "sinless perfection" this side of death? Theoretically, I can't think of a reason why not; but I don't know how we could ever really know whether someone has reached it unless we're God. If there are Christians who

59

have done it since Christ walked the earth (and they knew it for sure), their humility has likely kept them from sharing this news.

MOVING YOUR FEET

In the first chapter of Joshua, God promised to give the land of Canaan to the Israelites. But God also instructed them that they must go in and *take over* the land that was being given to them. "I am giving you every place where you set foot, exactly as I promised Moses," God told Joshua (Joshua 1:3). If the Israelites hadn't moved their feet, they wouldn't have been able to live in the land God was giving them.

Holiness is like that. God has made us holy through Jesus, and we have to move our feet to see the fruition. But as we do this, it's good to remember these words of John Wesley: "Even perfect holiness is acceptable to God only through Jesus Christ."[3]

So with all this in mind, let us go be holy . . . because God is holy (1 Peter 1:16).

Amen.

---

3. From "A Plain Account of Christian Perfection," by John Wesley in *The Works of John Wesley,* Volume 11, Number 29, (Zondervan, 1872), edited by Thomas Jackson; pages 366–446. *http:// wesley.nnu.edu/john-wesley/a-plain-account-of-christian-perfection.* Accessed 26 February 2014.

QUESTIONS

1. What is "being glad in the Lord" (Philippians 3:1)?

2. Why does Paul bring up all of his assets? Why does he then say that he's writing them off (Philippians 3:5-6)?

3. Describe the righteousness that Paul says he has found (Philippians 3:9). How do we find that righteousness?

4. What does it mean to be conformed to the death of Jesus (Philippians 3:10)?

5. What is the "resurrection of the dead" that Paul mentions in Philippians 3:11? How certain is he that he's going to reach it? How does this relate to believers today?

6. What does Paul mean by "being perfected" (Philippians 3:12)? How are we perfected today?

7. What do you think Philippians 3:16 means? How do we carry this out?

8. Describe the relationship between love and holiness.

9. Do you believe that it's possible for a Christian to reach perfection in this life? Why, or why not?

CONVERGE

Bible Studies

NEW TITLES!

ENCOUNTERING GRACE
by Joseph Yoo
9781426795534

IDOLATRY
by Curtis Zackery
9781426795541

CRIES OF THE POOR
by Grace Biskie
9781426795558

And more to come!

FASTING
by Ashlee Alley
9781426795565

Previously released!

WOMEN OF THE BIBLE
by James A. Harnish
9781426771545

OUR COMMON SINS
by Dottie Escobedo-Frank
9781426768989

WHO YOU ARE IN CHRIST
by Shane Raynor
9781426771538

SHARING THE GOSPEL
by Curtis Zackery
9781426771569

KINGDOM BUILDING
by Grace Biskie
9781426771576

PRACTICAL PRAYER
by Joseph Yoo
9781426778254

RECLAIMING ANGER
by David Dorn
9781426771552

THREE GIFTS, ONE CHRIST
by Katie Z. Dawson
9781426778278

WHO IS JESUS?
by Adam Thomas
9781426778292

PERPLEXING SCRIPTURES
by Josh Tinley
9781426789533

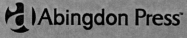

Abingdon Press

BKM146600009 PACP01474728-01

CPSIA information can be obtained at www.ICGtesting.com
Printed in the USA
LVOW05s1220120314

376963LV00003B/5/P